# KIND MIND

## Volume 1
### 10 Tools To Motivate Positive Thinking

I0558368

**Hues Productions**

# *KIND MIND*
## *VOLUME 2*

**COPYRIGHT © 2024 by Hues Productions**
First Edition ~ April 2024
Updated Version ~ February 2026

*Author: Hues Productions*

*Executive Editor: B. Hughes*

*Concept developed by B. Hughes of Hues Productions*

 KINDMINDBOOK@GMAIL.COM

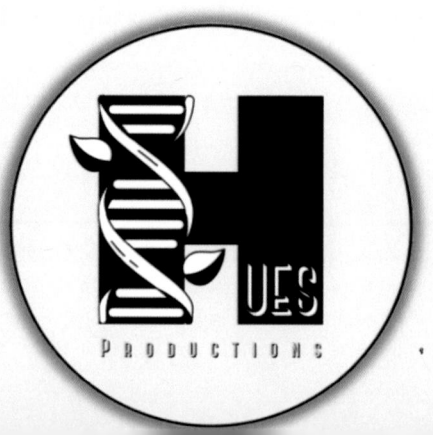

# PREFACE

Kind Mind, is a gift of love from Hues Productions. Let me start by reminding you that YOU are wonderful. I am grateful for you.

I strive to bring awareness to the importance of discussing ways to normalize being kind to your mind. I fell in love with experiencing the benefits of exploring holistic ways to help with my own mental health. So much so, that I want to share some tools that have helped me, specifically with you.

I know firsthand how challenging it can be to keep positive thoughts. Especially in the midst of hard times. Kind Mind encourages you with tools of knowledge for your journey.

# ACKNOWLEDGMENTS

I am infinitely grateful to the Most High, for all that is and all that will be. I am honored to be who I am and whose I am.

An everlasting thank you to my mother and father. Thank you for planting "good soil" for me to grow in.

A very special thank you to the person who motivates me to be the best "me" I can be.
My amazing son, Mason.
It is such a joy to have you in this life.

Also, a huge thank you to one of my truest friends. Thank you Yoyo for being the light that you are and extending your wisdom and guidance in my life. Your friendship and support is forever appreciated.

# CONTENTS

# INTRODUCTION

Thank you for reading this.

Your decision to motivate a positive mindset is worth acknowledging.

This book is to inspire you with tools to help keep a kind mind.

Keep growing.

You've got this.

# Rest

Rest is powerful. One of my personal favorites.
Many of us honestly just don't seem to get enough rest. A lack of rest showed up in my life as anxiety, stress, and just flat-out being tired. Think of resting, like charging your body. Getting enough sleep will reboot your mind, help improve your mood and allow your nervous system time to relax. Reset.

**Rest is an effective mental wellness tool.**

We have all heard our doctors and parents tell us to make sure we get enough sleep. Circumstances in our lives can sometimes complicate our ability to prioritize sleeping. Everyone differs. Allow yourself time to rest - for as long as you need to. When you feel you've rested enough, you're more likely to feel ready for the day mentally.

# TOOL ONE
# Rest

**PRIORITIZE GETTING ENOUGH REST**

Have you ever taken a nap and woke up irritable? Or, went to rest but couldn't fall asleep? Next thing you know, your alarm goes off and it feels like you didn't really rest at all. That could be your mind's reaction to a lack of sleep. I recommend occasionally trying uninterrupted rest. No alarms, no one shaking you awake. Just a natural awakening. That is your mind's way of letting you know it has had enough rest. I wake up in a much better mood when I can indulge in alarm-less rest. I feel refreshed when I can rest without the distractions of the outside world. Test this theory, and give it a try! Go to bed without TV, without a phone, just silence and let your body wake up on its own. If you sleep with a partner, let them know as well so that they can support your uninterrupted rest.

Show your mind some love by resting well.

## TOOL TWO
# Practice Gratitude

**START EACH DAY WITH GRATITUDE**

Now that you've rested well. That moment right when your body wakes up, try taking a moment to give thanks for the day. Say it in your mind, say it with a smile, or say it out loud if you want! Do what authentically comes from a place of being grateful for a new day. For a while now, I've made a conscious choice to say "thank you" before doing anything else when I first wake up.

**Why this works**

This isn't one of the tools that you will notice immediately. The more you use it, the more you'll understand. It is like prepping the day for positivity. Every thought of what you are grateful for creates a kind mind. It helps to acknowledge the good things in your life.

# TOOL TWO
# Practice Gratitude

You probably use this tool more often than you think. In some cultures, we call it giving thanks. Gratitude is a feeling of thankfulness, reminding yourself that good things do exist in your life.

I was advised by one of my therapists to write down things I was thankful for. It reminded me that the small things matter too. Actually, the small things mattered most. My list grew bigger and bigger until I had pages long of things I was grateful for. I even wrote things in advance that I claim to come. Say it, write it, feel it, draw it, think it, whatever feels best for you.

**ACTIVITIES FOR THIS TOOL:**
AFFIRMATIONS
POSITIVE MANTRAS
SHOW APPRECIATION
JOURNAL
WRITE DOWN WHAT YOU ARE THANKFUL FOR
ACTS OF SERVICE
SHARE & GIVE BACK

# Practice Gratitude

**EXAMPLES:**

I am thankful for sunshine, family, and good friends.

I am grateful for good health.

I am grateful for the movement of my limbs.

I am thankful for life.

I am well.

Think of a mantra that you can remind yourself of.

I repeat phrases like this in my mind or out loud throughout the day, not only to affirm myself but, to show gratitude.

# **Practice Gratitude**

**MORE EXAMPLES THAT I USE**

I feel loved

I understand myself

I love growing

I create great things

I speak life

I see healing

Make it a part of your daily routine to think or say positive things about yourself, every day.

# TOOL THREE
# the Present

If showing gratitude is a challenge, focusing on the present can be a good place to start. Take a moment. Put a pause on thoughts. Just focus on the right now. Take a few deep breaths. When I want to focus on the present, I let go of any second before right now. Even in hard times, those hard times are a part of your growing process. Everyone makes mistakes. Let go of any judgments or expectations.

Allowing your thoughts to linger too long in the past can overwhelm your mind and cause negative thoughts. Yet, when I thought too much into the future, this would show up negatively as anxiety. I found that when I took a deep breath, slowed down my thoughts, and started to focus only on "right now" - I was able to find a balance. With this tool, I gained a better understanding of the importance of appreciating the gift of the present.

# TOOL THREE
# the Present

**GIFT OF FOCUSING ON THE PRESENT**
Right now, you are alive. That is the present truth.
Take a moment with me.
Close your eyes and focus on your breaths.

Think of the present like breathing. You don't have to remind yourself to take a breath. It just happens, just like the present.

Deep breathing and meditation are other great ways to practice this tool. For me, the idea of mindfulness starts with pausing the world on the outside and pulling into the you on the inside. I see it as an act of practicing consciousness.

When you focus on the present you can start thriving. All of the answers you seek are already inside of you, right now, in the present. Come home to yourself - pause, breathe, and allow yourself to **be present**.

# TOOL FOUR
# Face it

## FEEL YOUR FEELINGS, ALL THE WAY THROUGH.

Life isn't only about good times. Coming from someone who has made it through many hard times, the rough times have just as much of an impact. I would often run from my issues. I'd push it so far to the back of my mind that I would end up prolonging the pain of that situation. I couldn't run from my problems forever. Eventually, I had to stop dwelling on it and "face it". Yes, that situation sucked. So. I was determined to turn it around. If I couldn't, I wanted to change my perspective on it (1). **I tried to understand what my emotions were telling me vs trying to control the emotion**.

Hard times are meant to build and prepare us for the next phases of life. Challenging times are inevitable. How you react when they show up in life is up to you. You have the power to control how you react. This tool helps to avoid dwelling on issues and encourages you to identify and face them head-on.

# TOOL FOUR
# Face it

**LET'S PRACTICE...**
Write down those negative thoughts.
CHALLENGE THEM. Take one thought at a time.
Sit in it. Observe what the negative thought is trying to convey. Is it stemming from fear, lack of the unknown, or bad experiences? Identify it. Now, throw some facts at it. Consider counteracting those thoughts with something realistic or positive. **Don't judge what you feel with this tool**. However, be prepared to go through your emotions fully as you utilize this tool. Don't hold back.

Challenge a negative thought by  considering,
*"Is this thought actually true?"*.

If not, throw it away. Reject it immediately in your mind. Replace worry or doubt with fact-checking those thoughts.

If so, focus your thoughts on ways to change it, or accept it. You create your reality, with your mind.

# TOOL FIVE
# Acceptance

**"IT IS, WHAT IT IS"**

"It is, what it is" is a phrase I would hear quite often in my community growing up. I never really grasped the depth of this wisdom until I was older. What is yours, is yours. What is meant for you, is just for you. What isn't for you, just isn't for you. It is what it is.

We all have our own paths to travel. I find it easier to let go and allow peace to fill my mind when I begin to accept things for what they are. To me, acceptance is that feeling when you are not angry. You don't feel resentment. No doubt, no expectations, no worry, no fear. No judgment. Just acceptance.

Acceptance isn't dismissing the situation. It isn't convincing yourself it doesn't exist. It can be difficult to accept our circumstances sometimes. This tool of total acceptance is acknowledging that it is just that - what it is. Even people. Accept people for who they are - not who you want them to be.

# TOOL FIVE
# Acceptance

The way you interpret something controls how you react to it. Our thoughts truly become our reality. If you interpret things in a light of: "I can accept _____", then you reroute thoughts toward a neutral foundation.

Practice using this tool with accountability, boundaries, and discernment. If a negative thought is something you have the ability to change, then make a plan toward positive change. Do not accept negative thoughts that you can change. If it does not align with your goals and is in your control, let it go. For things that may be out of your control, try accepting it for what it is.

Most importantly,
**a c c e p t**
**y o u r s e l f .**

# Compassion

## PRACTICE SELF- COMPASSION

We often are way too hard on ourselves. Have compassion for yourself. You may be experiencing something new, trying to learn the lesson in mistakes, or just going through everyday living.

Let go of judgment.
Validate your feelings.
Embrace forgiveness for yourself.

You don't always have to be strong.
You don't always have to be happy.
It's okay to mess up. It's okay to cry.
It's okay to be hurt. It's okay to not know what to do.
It's okay to change your mind. It's okay to not be okay.

**Be extremely mindful of the way that you speak about yourself in your mind and verbally.**

Your mind is listening too.
Show yourself compassion.

# TOOL SIX
# Compassion

Now that you have a full cup of compassion, extend that overflow of grace to others. A good way to show compassion is to practice empathy. Put yourself in their shoes or pull from your memory, what someone may be experiencing. We all feel the same emotions. We all are learning to navigate through life at our own speed. Showing empathy is an ancient practice that helps us stay connected as spiritual beings going through this human experience. You never know what someone else may be going through.

**PRACTICE NOT TAKING THINGS PERSONALLY** (2)

I know I know - easier said than done, right? Trust me, this works. How someone treats you is rarely ever about you. How they treat you is a reflection of themselves. When you offer compassion to someone, even if they don't deserve it at that moment, it benefits you. Viewing others with compassion helps bring peace of mind.

# the Company You Keep

## BE MINDFUL OF THE COMPANY YOU KEEP
(Pro 13:20) (3)

This ancient proverb is a teaching of many generations. It teaches the importance of carefully choosing the company you keep. Along my journey, I have gained a new understanding of this wisdom as a kind mind tool. You have the right to be selective about who gets access to you. Don't be afraid to walk away from people that may be negative influences. I find it wise to be guarded and mindful of the company you keep.

## YOU BECOME THE COMPANY YOU KEEP
 (1 Co 15:33) (4)

Simple, yet powerful. Having positive energy around you is therapeutic. Surround yourself with positive people that inspire you. That influence will eventually rub off onto you. The same is true for negativity. If you surround yourself with negativity, it will influence you as well. Observe the garden your mind grows in with this tool.

# TOOL SEVEN
## the Company You Keep

This tool has had a major impact on my life. I started by setting boundaries for myself. Anything outside of YOUR boundaries, leave on the outside. Identify clearly what your boundaries are and DO NOT compromise on them. It is 100% okay to separate yourself from negativity to keep a kind mind. Even if it is family or friends, coworkers or strangers.

Our brains are stimulated by the information it receives every day. Overstimulating your mind with things that aren't so positive can affect the way you think. Social media, music, shows, news stations, movies, video games, and negative people pollute our brains at times.

Take a break from anything that brings negativity if you are trying to keep a kind mind. Your surroundings also strongly influence your mind. Not just people.

# What Makes YOU Happy

**DO WHATEVER MAKES YOU HAPPY**

Doing things that you enjoy contributes to creating a kind mind. **Prioritize the things that YOU enjoy.**

For this tool, I recommend writing a list. Take time to think about what makes you happy. Then, look at your list - and smile. You hack your mind every time you smile. Just as the brain sends signals to the body, the body also sends signals to the brain. Smiling or thinking of something that makes you happy is a hack that I love.

Think of things that aren't just materialistic.
For example, some things on my list are trying new things, being in the sun, learning, fun activities, writing, good music, creating, and showing kindness to others.

Science shows that our brains release different chemicals that influence us.

# What Makes YOU Happy

This tool helps to naturally boost powerful brain chemicals like endorphins, dopamine, serotonin, and oxytocin.

Ever wondered how looking at someone you love can almost instantly relax you? **Endorphins.** Laughter, time with good company, being outdoors, or just doing something you love doing releases this chemical in your brain (5).

**Dopamine** is known as the reward chemical and helps you feel motivated (5). Eating well, self-care activities, getting something done, or celebrating you, this chemical releases that "yeah, I did that!" feeling.

**Serotonin** is the mood chemical that helps you feel positive and relaxed (5). Meditation can boost serotonin. Even simply believing in yourself promotes this chemical.

**Oxytocin** helps keep you connected. Hug someone, give a compliment, socialize, or bond with others for a long-lasting "happy" feeling of natural oxytocin (5).

# Self-Care

**POUR INTO YOU**

Self-care is the most satisfying tool that I use in my *Kind Mind* toolbox.

Doing good things for yourself is not only good for your brain, but good for others too. You can't pour from an empty cup. Refill your own cup with this tool.

**You must pour love, compassion, acceptance, and grace into yourself first.**

It isn't selfish to be self-full.

I call it my "me time". By taking time to provide for your own needs and desires, you practice self-care. I find a sense of clarity and confidence when I practice this tool.

# TOOL NINE
# **Self-Care**

Self-care is beneficial to your mind. Practice doing things that put a pause on distractions and allow you to focus on feeding your well-being. Self-care can be as simple as a bath or as extravagant as a vacation. However you do it, do it for YOU.

Self-care helps you feel good about yourself from the inside, out. When you take care of yourself, you'll feel more empowered.

**Care for yourself, unapologetically**.
Forgive yourself.
Love yourself.
Date yourself.
Treat yourself.
Teach yourself.
Invest in yourself.
Take care of yourself.

# TOOL TEN
# HELP

## HELP YOURSELF, SEEK HELP

All too often, people suffer in silence. All because they were too afraid to ask for help. I've been there before. It was the "how" that often would challenge me. If you are struggling with your mental health, I believe it is wise to seek help. I encourage talking to someone that you trust or seeking professional help. I learned that I had to ask for help when I needed it and accepted the fact that I was **never alone**.

Much of the advice that I am able to share with you today is because I asked for help when I needed it.
I learned to not be ashamed to ask for help and to not be disappointed if I didn't receive the help I needed. The knowledge I gained in seeking help, has contributed greatly to my *Kind Mind* toolbox.

Professional help can support a path to mental wellness. For me, an unbiased mental health professional helped share education on managing symptoms of my particular mental health conditions.

# TOOL TEN
# HELP

Utilizing professional help as **a tool** and **not THE answer**, is a strong point of view that I advocate.

I find that it offers options for treating symptoms that I experienced. Cognitive Behavioral Therapy is a holistic style that I have found works well for me. Even if therapy isn't your cup of tea, seeking professional help can identify if you may have a mental health condition. Healthy coping skills vary for each situation and each individual. Expanding your toolbox with knowledge of professional help can also influence a kind mind. Whether you prefer holistic guidance, lifestyle changes, belief systems, science, or healthcare guidance, I recommend seeking help when needed. You deserve to feel heard. You deserve to feel valued.

**You are important.** If you are struggling with your mental health, please seek help.

# CONCLUSION

Give yourself permission to **REST**. Just as your body needs a break, so does your brain. Once you're awake, remember to show **GRATITUDE**. We can combat negativity by showing thankfulness. Forgive your past and live in **THE PRESENT** for a better future. When having negative thoughts - **FACE IT**. Negativity comes around us whether we like it or not. YOU have the power to control how you react to it. Your thoughts about yourself become your reality. So believe in yourself, in all that you do. Challenge negative thoughts with facts. **ACCEPTANCE** is a powerful tool when used the right way. No matter what happens, it is a part of your purpose and growth. Be patient with yourself & give yourself grace. Have **COMPASSION** for your journey and the you that is still learning. Using compassion for yourself to motivate positive thinking can help you be kind to others in return. You become **THE COMPANY YOU KEEP.** Being mindful of the people you surround yourself with strongly influences how you think. Do **WHAT MAKES YOU HAPPY** but create & uphold your boundaries. You're responsible for your happiness and can naturally release "feel good" chemicals to your mind. I recommend prioritizing time for yourself to do what makes you happy. This kind of **SELF-CARE** allows you to pour into yourself and fulfill your own needs. We all go through different things at different stages of life. Remember, you are not alone. I have found it helpful to seek **HELP** when needed. Keep going. Be kind to your mind. Keep growing.

I am
I feel
I have
I love
I speak
I see
I know

# NOTES

(1)

Angelou, M. (1994). *Wouldn't Take Nothing For My Journey Now* (p. 87).
Bantam Books.

(2)

Ruiz, M. (1997). *The Four Agreements: A Toltec Wisdom Book* (pp. 47-49).
Amber-Allen Publishing.

(3)

*The Ethiopic Holy Bible. containing the entire canon of the Ethiopian Bible.*
(2007) (Vol. 1). Saderingrad Productions.

(4)

*The Complete Jewish Bible: An English version of the Tanakh and B'rit Hadashah.*
(1998). Jewish New Testament Publications.

(5)

Dfarhud, D., Malmir, M., & Khanahmadi, M. (2014, November). Happiness &
Health: The biological factors- systematic review article. Iranian journal of
public health. https://www.ncbi.nlm.nih.gov/pmc/articles/PMC4449495/